BIOLOGICAL, NUCLEAR, & CHEMICAL WEAPONS

FIGHTING TERRORISM

David Baker

www.rourkepublishing.com

PHOTO CREDITS: pp. 6, 39: AFP/Getty Images; p. 16 (t): Andrea Booher/FEMA News Photo; p. 23 (t): Robert Cameron/Stone/Getty Images; pp.12, 18: Corbis; p. 23 (b): Digital Globe/Getty Images; p. 31: Chris Fairclough Worldwide Ltd; p. 4: Files/AFP/Getty Images; p. 26: Keystone/ Getty Images; p. 15: Junji Kurokawa/AFP/Getty Images; p. 25: National Archives/ Time & Life Pictures/Getty Images; p. 32: Gerry Penny/AFP/Getty Images; p. 29: Aamir Qureshi/AFP/Getty Images; p. 19: Stone/Getty Images; p. 27: STR/AFP/ Getty Images; p. 36: Alex Wong/ Getty Images; p. 21: Vassily Yegorov/Central Press/Getty Images; p. 37: Zufarov/AFP/ Getty Images; pp. 8 (Senior Airman Staci Clapper), 16 (b) (Senior Airman Jeffrey Allen), 22 (Staff Sgt. Steven Pearsall): U.S. Air Force; pp. 7, 9: U.S. Army Photo/LOC; p. 42: PA3 Mike Hvozda/U.S. Coast Guard; pp. 41 (James Tourtellotte), 43 (Gerald Nino): U.S. Customs and Border Protection; p. 14 (Master Sgt. Edward D. Kniery): U.S. Marine Corps; pp. 33 (Journalist 3rd Class Stephen P. Weaver), 35 (Photographer's Mate 2nd Class Jeffrey Lehrberg): U.S. Navy; p. 10: U.S. Signal Corps/LOC

Title page picture shows troops on a biological, chemical, and nuclear weapons exercise.

Produced for Rourke Publishing by Discovery Books
Editor: Paul Humphrey
Designer: Ian Winton
Photo researcher: Rachel Tisdale

Library of Congress Cataloging-in-Publication Data

Baker, David, 1944-
    Biological, nuclear, and chemical weapons / by David Baker.
        p. cm. -- (Fighting terrorism)
    Includes index.
    ISBN 1-59515-489-2
    1. Terrorism--United States--Prevention--Juvenile literature. 2. Weapons of mass destruction--Juvenile literature. 3. Biological weapons--Juvenile literature. 4. Nuclear weapons--Juvenile literature. 3. Chemical weapons--Juvenile literature. I. Title. II. Series.
    HV6432.B33 2006
    363.320973--dc22

                                 2005028173

Printed in the USA

TABLE OF CONTENTS

Chapter One

Weapons of Mass Destruction

Throughout the long history of human conflict, warriors have sought the best weapons, the most effective means of winning, and the quickest ways to destroy their enemies. For several thousand years rulers and kings looked to gain military advantages over their foes. They employed **alchemists** to conjure up explosives that could set objects on fire, they forged new steels to make better swords, and they made bigger bows to shoot arrows greater distances.

The search for the ultimate weapon to use in war or as a **deterrent** has occupied the time and money of national leaders around the world for centuries. In the modern age the nature of conflict has changed, and now it is scientists and engineers who are able to create the ultimate weapons.

Science has expanded human knowledge to an amazing level, and today the very substance of matter itself is understood. During the last century alone scientists unlocked the secrets of the atom and the universe. This information can be used for beneficial purposes or it can be used for destruction.

Chemists have explored the nature of elements and can produce substances unknown in the natural world. Poisons and **toxic** substances manufactured by chemists can break down the ability of living things to survive.

Biologists have explored the way living things are made and can explain the evolution of life. Yet they can also produce biological agents that are able to destroy much human life. **Physicists** have split the atom and explored the universe with

(Opposite) A French nuclear weapons test at Mururoa Atoll in the Pacific, 1971. Such weapons could, in the hands of terrorists, have devastating consequences.

In 1866 a Swedish scientist named Alfred Nobel invented dynamite, which he hoped would be used for landscaping and breaking up rocks. He was so horrified that it was being used for war that he set up a prize in 1901 that is awarded annually for outstanding contributions in chemistry, physics, medicine, literature, economics, and peace.

telescopes. They have also made nuclear bombs with more explosive capacity than their inventors could ever have imagined.

Over the last century scientists have worked with engineers to develop a terrifying range of modern weapons that use the substance of matter to bring death and destruction. Some weapons built for military use are so horrific that they have never been used in war.

Alfred Nobel invented dynamite, but he only wanted it put to peaceful uses.

The Japanese city of Hiroshima was flattened by the atom bomb dropped on August 6, 1945.

Chemical, biological, and nuclear devices for defense or deterrent purposes are called Weapons of Mass Destruction (WMD), and they have a frightening relevance for us all. Weapons of mass destruction are those that can result in the death of millions of people in a single application.

One firefighter checks another's chemical protection suit during an exercise. Firefighters will be at the forefront in the event of a chemical attack on the United States.

Because we live in a world where terrorists are prepared to use anything they can get their hands on to bring death and destruction to innocent people, the possibility that they might use weapons of mass destruction is ever present.

The U.S. government has taken extraordinary steps to protect its citizens from the possibility of such an attack, and our federal and state emergency services are equipped to handle an attack by terrorists using chemical, biological, or nuclear weapons.

(Opposite) This photo shows U.S. soldiers suffering a gas attack during World War I. This was probably taken during a training exercise.

Chapter Two

Chemical Attack

If terrorists attack using chemical weapons, they can use any one of a range of different substances. Each has its own application but all can cause extensive suffering and death. Chemical weapons were first used in World War I (1914-1918).

Known as "gas," (actually vapor or **aerosols** of toxic substances), it consisted of commercial chemicals used for killing vermin.

The Germans were the first to use gas; they merely opened large canisters of chlorine and let it drift downwind across the

American troops on gas mask drill at Scott Field, Illinois, during World War II.

enemy battle lines. In 1917 they started using mustard gas shells fired from guns and thrown behind the enemy positions. The gas was able to penetrate a wide range of materials including leather and fabric.

Mustard gas created painful burns on the skin and could cause blindness. It was considered so terrible a weapon that it was banned in 1925. However, several countries used chemical weapons in the 1930s including Italy in Ethiopia and Japan in Manchuria and China.

Before World War II (1939-45), chemical weapons were made from standard chemicals manufactured by commercial companies. With the outbreak of war, several countries began to develop more sophisticated chemical weapons. One example was **phosgene**, a relatively simple substance that irritates the eyes and chokes the respiratory tract. Phosgene is important in industry as a chlorinating chemical used to kill bacteria.

FACT FILE ★

Because large stocks of gas and liquid nerve agents were held by several countries during the Cold War (1945-1991), the possibility that they may have been used encouraged research into ways to protect against them. The United States and Great Britain held very large stocks of these agents, and laboratories in both countries produced valuable research into ways their effects on the general public could be minimized. This research has more recently been used by our emergency aid services.

Another example was hydrogen cyanide, known as a blood agent. When applied in large doses it keeps oxygen from reaching the tissues of the body. All these chemicals were known as "poor men's weapons," because a modern fighting force could give soldiers protection against them.

No gas was used on the battlefield during World War II, but it was used against Jewish and other prisoners in German extermination camps. This photo shows prisoners from one of those camps during their liberation in 1945.

Today there are many more types of even more lethal chemical agents. They belong to a category known as nerve agents. These block **enzymes** that are necessary for the proper functioning of the nervous system. They are in liquid form at room temperature and include a particularly harmful product known as **sarin**, discovered in 1938 by Gerhard Schrader, a German scientist.

Fortunately the Germans never used sarin or any other chemical weapons during World War II. Sarin is one of the most effective weapons on respiratory systems, and the United States and the Soviet Union went into full-scale production with this after the war.

The results of using these nerve agents would have been so horrific that neither country wanted to be the first to use them. They were true deterrents because there was little defense against them and therefore no way of stopping them affecting forces on both sides.

Nevertheless, although no chemical weapons were used for fear of retaliation, several countries including Germany, Russia, the United States, and Great Britain produced such vast quantities of chemical weapons that there was a problem getting rid of them when the war ended.

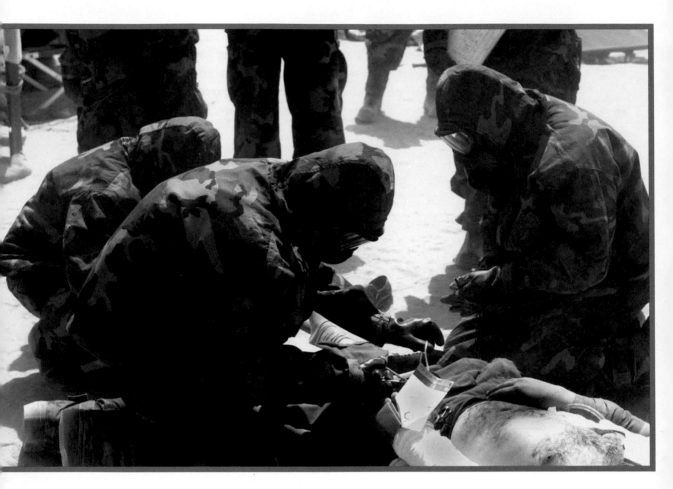

During a chemical attack alert in Iraq, U.S. Navy hospital personnel treat a wounded enemy prisoner of war as part of Operation Iraqi Freedom, March 2003.

Old ships were filled with the chemical agents and taken out to the deepest parts of the ocean and sunk! Given our current greater environmental concerns, that solution would never happen today.

Chemical weapons have never been used in wars involving the major powers, but they were used by Iraq's Saddam Hussein against Iranian soldiers during the 1982-1987 Iran-Iraq war. Because chemical weapons spread so quickly, they affected large numbers of young children and women caught in the conflict.

Also, because the chemicals have such terrible effects, causing lengthy pain and, usually, a painful and agonizing death, these weapons appeal to fanatics and terrorists.

There have been several attempts to use sarin gas and other nerve agents to spread terror and panic. Extreme cult gangs in Japan succeeded in spreading nerve agents through the air conditioning system of Tokyo subway trains in a March 1995 attack. They were arrested and tried as criminals. The knowledge they had has been taken up by other terrorists.

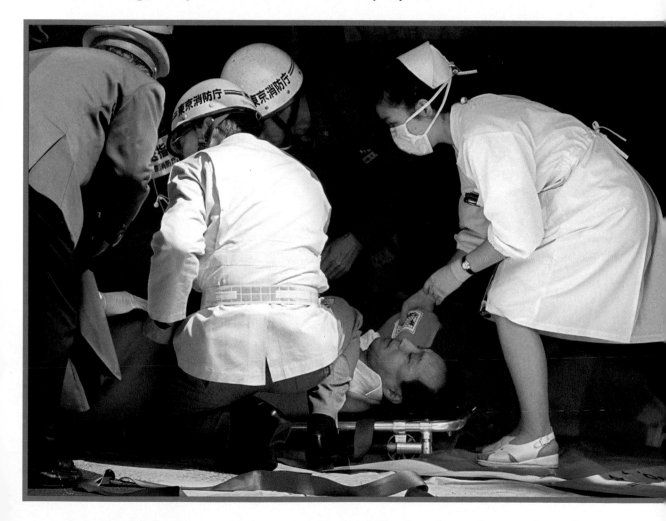

A commuter is given emergency treatment following the sarin attack on the Tokyo subway, March 1995.

Firefighters search through the wreckage following the Al Qaeda terrorist attacks on New York City, September 11, 2001. Since then, intelligence operations have suggested that Al Qaeda is on the lookout for chemical weapons.

Intelligence operations carried out since 9/11 have revealed that the Al Qaeda terrorist organization run by Osama bin Laden has made strong efforts to obtain nerve agents and to use them against targets in the United States and in European countries.

A chemical attack joint exercise taking place between the forces of the United States and the Republic of South Korea.

Chapter Three

Biological Warfare

Throughout history there have been many examples where infectious diseases caused significant impact on military operations. The intentional **dissemination** of disease adds a completely new threat to that posed already by infections and toxins. The value to a military force in distributing such harmful compounds has attracted their use on several occasions—but only to a limited degree.

The advanced research into biological products and the way they can be made more lethal became a significant part of weapons development during the Cold War. Researchers in laboratories in the United States and elsewhere worked hard to understand the range of biological products that could be used in war to enable them to find ways of protecting soldiers and civilians.

This research showed that it would be possible to perform **genetic** engineering for both chemical and biological weapons. Genes can be introduced into a **virulent** cell by adding strands of DNA (the genetic code) that amplified their effects a hundred times. Genetic **modification** can make biological strains that are

A hospital tent for Union troops during the Civil War. In previous centuries, disease often killed more troops in a war than fighting on the battlefield.

resistant to extremes of temperature, ultraviolet radiation, and dehydration. It can also alter non-toxic cells to produce toxins. Conversely, it is possible to neutralize toxins to produce **vaccines**.

Biological agents are divided into various classes. Any one of them can be turned into a terrorist's weapon. For this reason, scientists have to categorize them carefully to identify types and sources. Bacteria are free-living organisms that may grow on

Bacteria are tiny living organisms that can only be seen with the aid of a microscope. This makes them a very attractive weapon for terrorists. This photo shows deadly anthrax bacteria on human tissue, highly magnified.

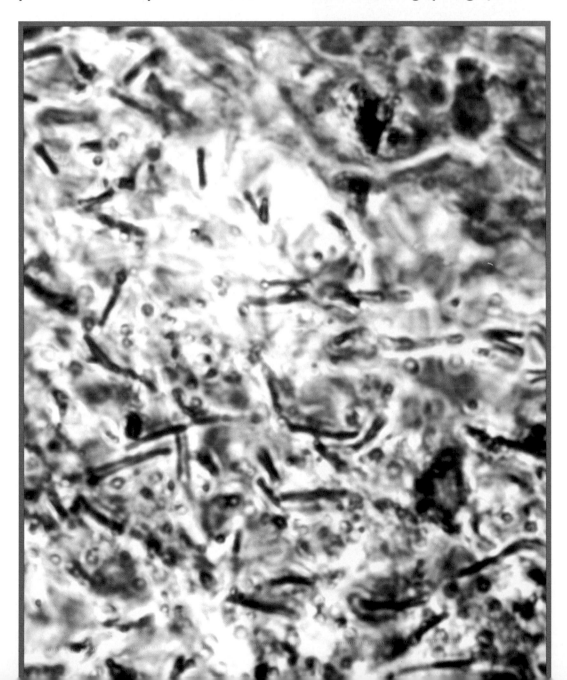

Anthrax is a serious disease caused by bacteria. It most commonly affects cattle, sheep, and goats, but it can be passed to humans when they are exposed to infected animals.

Anthrax can pass into humans through cuts in the skin, through eating contaminated meat or by breathing in the bacteria. In the first two instances, the disease is usually treatable. However, for people who breathe in the bacteria, the chances of survival are very small indeed.

Anthrax is an attractive weapon for the terrorist because nearly 3 billion lethal doses are contained in just one ounce of anthrax material. It is also cheap and easy to produce, store, and make into weapons.

solid or liquid cultures, but they can be destroyed by **antibiotics**.

Viruses are organisms that need living cells in order to **replicate** and do not respond to antibiotics. **Rickettsiae** are tiny organisms that show behavior similar to both bacteria and viruses, but they too grow only within living cells. Chlamydia are parasites that hop from cell to cell. Fungi are primitive plants that draw nutrition from decaying vegetable matter and do not need light or oxygen.

Finally, toxins are poisonous substances produced from living plants, animals, or very small organisms. All these classes of biological agents threaten to bring disease and infection on a massive scale. They can be manipulated to boost their strength and modified to enhance their danger.

Scientists deliberately boost some biological agents, and research into disease and methods of prevention is important to fighting these

During the Cold War the Soviets liked to parade their arsenal of weapons through the streets of Moscow.

where they occur naturally. A lot of experience was gained during the Cold War when it was feared that the Soviet Union might use biological weapons in time of war. With the development of vaccines to counteract the effects, special analyzers were produced to provide instant identification of the agent concerned.

Our troops are trained to be ready to protect citizens in the event of a biological or chemical attack.

For fighting troops, special protective garments were designed that allowed them to remain unharmed long enough to evacuate the area. This knowledge is used today in preparing for public safety should terrorists ever mount an attack using biological agents.

In a world where terrorists seek to gain the possession of any weapon capable of inflicting harm to innocent people, the existence of biological weapons increases the threat and the potential harm they can cause. Unlike chemical agents, biological weapons spread uncontrollably throughout living things. It is very difficult to stop them and almost impossible to put a barrier on how far they reach out from the point of contamination. They can quite easily affect the **perpetrator** as well as the **victim**.

(Above) The Hoover Dam in Nevada. The nation's water supplies are a likely target for biological or chemical attack.

(Right) This satellite image was taken in October 2002. It was at the time believed to be of a bioweapons research facility in Iraq.

Chapter Four

Nuclear Nightmare

Research into atomic weapons began early in the 20th century, when British scientists split the atom and proved that matter held extraordinary amounts of energy. Under the right circumstances, this energy could be unleashed either in a controlled and slow way to drive turbines for electricity production or all at once, creating a massive explosion.

When the United States joined the war against Japan and Germany in December 1941, U.S. and British scientists teamed up to build an atom bomb. The first atomic explosion took place on July 16, 1945, at Alamagordo, New Mexico. It produced a blast equal to 20,000 tons (18,200 metric tons) of high explosive. The biggest conventional bomb then available weighed about 10 tons (9 metric tons).

The first two atomic bombs were dropped on the Japanese cities of Hiroshima and Nagasaki in August 1945, and by the end of the month the Japanese had indicated they would accept unconditional surrender.

Beginning in the 1950s both the Soviet Union and the United States developed a much more powerful weapon—the hydrogen

A nuclear weapons test in the 1950s is observed by U.S. Army troops.

bomb. An atom bomb works by splitting atoms apart. This is
known as a "fission" bomb. A hydrogen bomb works by
slamming particles together so that they fuse. This led to the

term "fusion" bomb. Nuclear fusion releases much greater amounts of energy than nuclear fission. Atom bombs are limited to an explosive force equal to about 100,000 tons (91,000 metric tons). A hydrogen bomb can release a force equal to millions of tons of high explosives **detonated** at one time.

Since the attacks on Japan in 1945, no nuclear bomb has been dropped in anger although there have been almost 2,100 tests in the atmosphere, under the sea, and under the ground. In 1962 an atmospheric test ban outlawed tests in the atmosphere. This

President John F. Kennedy (center) signs the nuclear test ban treaty in 1962.

is because nuclear weapons release long-lived radiation that at the very least seriously affects human health and at worst kills in a most painful and agonizing manner.

The levels of radiation were noticeable in the atmosphere and the build-up would have had a measurable effect on human life. From 1962 underground explosions became the only way nuclear devices could be tested. At that time the only nuclear powers were the United States, the Soviet Union, the United Kingdom, France, and China.

A Shaheen II ballistic missile is launched in Pakistan. This weapon is capable of carrying a nuclear warhead deep into neighboring rival India.

Since then Israel, India, Pakistan, and North Korea all claim to have developed nuclear weapons. Iraq's former leader Saddam Hussein would have got them if he could have, and Iran says it is developing a nuclear capability. Now, Osama bin Laden says that he also has a right to nuclear weapons, and people from Al Qaeda have been going around the world trying to get them.

It is relatively easy to put a nuclear bomb together—if you have the components. The key product is the most difficult to get hold of. It is enriched uranium 235. The easiest way is to mine uranium ore from the ground and make it into a powder and soak it in sulfuric acid to **leach** out the pure uranium. It is then dried and filtered out into a coarse powder known as yellowcake. **Fluorine** gas is then blown through the yellowcake, and it is baked at 133° F (56° Celsius), converting it into a gas known as uranium hexafluoride.

Separation of the heavier atoms (U-238) from the lighter (U-235) is performed in a **centrifuge**. The lighter U-235 is then spun in a centrifuge 1,500 times, until it is about one-fifth pure. In this state it is known as highly enriched uranium-bomb grade material. This is converted to a metallic powder and molded into a sphere weighing 35 to 100 pounds (16 to 45 kg). It is now ready to be installed in a weapon. This is a simple device with an explosive force about equal to that of the bomb dropped on Hiroshima.

FACT FILE ★

Caught in early 2004, the head of Pakistan's nuclear weapons program, Abdul Qadeer Khan, traded nuclear secrets with Libya, Iran, and North Korea, making $400 million in the process. He organized parts from a uranium enrichment plant in South Africa, got designs for centrifuges from China, and got companies in Singapore, Spain, Germany, and Malaysia to make components for enrichment and for bomb-making.

Abdul Qadeer Khan traded Pakistan's nuclear secrets with Libya, Iran, and North Korea. However, he was never indicted, and in February 2004, he was officially pardoned by Pakistan's president.

A more exotic bomb, using a process that supports full-scale production of nuclear weapons, involves the reprocessing of plutonium extracted from spent nuclear fuel. This bomb needs a lot of money, huge resources, and factories and processing plants in large buildings that use high levels of electrical power and cooling water. It needs a nuclear reactor and a lot of knowledge and experience.

Yet this is the path taken by North Korea, a communist country opposed to democracy and free speech. Al Qaeda is known to have had talks with the Koreans, and Pakistani scientists have frequently met with both parties. Both Pakistan and North Korea are at present nuclear powers. It would not take much for Al Qaeda to get its hands on a bomb made by someone else or supplied by a sympathetic country.

Chapter Five

Trading in Death

Chemical and biological agents have an important role to play in daily life. Chemicals are produced in large quantities for use in the home, at work, and throughout our everyday lives. They are used for cleaning, for fertilizers to improve crops, for getting rid of germs, and to preserve food. In small quantities they are used for a wide range of activities.

Getting hold of the ingredients to make chemical weapons is easy and gives the terrorist little problem. Biological products are also in everyday life. They are important tools in treating sickness either in medication prescribed by a physician or in the more powerful agents used in hospital care.

Scientists in research laboratories around the nation use bacteria and viruses to conduct investigations into illnesses and disease to improve doctors' abilities to treat patients. Biological products are moved from one laboratory to another in the process of conducting investigations into their properties and the way they interact with each other.

Only in this way can biological products be used effectively in the fight against disease. Special precautions are taken to prevent these harmful agents from falling into the wrong hands, but it is easier for a terrorist to get hold of them than it is to make a nuclear weapon.

Terrorists have shown their eagerness to use anything possible to cause death and destruction and to bring panic and fear to innocent bystanders. Chemical, biological, and nuclear weapons are attractive to them because they have great potential for spreading alarm and for killing large numbers of people.

Because chemical and biological weapons are comparatively easy to get hold of they can be more useful to terrorists. This is because their effects are sustained over time and can spread

Many potentially dangerous chemicals are used for peaceful means, such as fertilizing crops.

The 2001 hoof-and-mouth disease outbreak in the United Kingdom showed how quickly disease could spread through the nation's livestock. Thousands of cattle and sheep had to be killed and burned.

panic. They can also be used to hit the national economy. Disease among cattle and pigs spreads quickly if unchecked promptly. Sickness in cattle can stop beef supplies, and diseases spread among animals can have a devastating economic effect.

One example of this was an accidental outbreak of hoof-and-mouth disease in the United Kingdom during 2001. Affecting cattle, sheep, and pigs, it resulted in several hundred thousand cattle and sheep being slaughtered and all supplies of beef being cut off from export. Only when the disease had been eradicated could the ban be lifted and exports were able to be shipped again. This cost the farmers and the British food industry the equivalent of tens of billions of dollars. Imagine what it would be like if diseases as simple as hoof-and-mouth disease were spread by terrorists around the nation, crippling food stocks and ruining the economy.

One worry is the frequent movement of chemical and biological products by ordinary transportation on road, rail, and by air. It is when these harmful products are on the move that they are most easily hijacked. There have been cases where products have disappeared, and some small quantities of lethal bacteria have never been found.

Nevertheless, chemical and biological materials are carefully logged in laboratories, in manufacturing plants for domestic

Italian firefighters dressed in chemical, biological, and radiological suits set up a circle of warning signs around a suspicious container during an exercise in April 2004.

products, and when being moved around. Special containers are sealed at the point of departure and records are maintained.

Inspectors from the Food and Drug Administration keep a tight watch on quantities produced, stocks held in factories and laboratories, and in the records when taken from place to place. Spot checks keep industrial and scientific users alert to the possibility of an instant raid by FDA officials with the threat of strong penalties and criminal charges if procedures are ignored.

This fight against terrorism is in the hands of health officials and government workers not usually associated with the drama of possible terrorist attack. Their work, however, is equally as vital as the air marshals who protect passengers on an airliner or the soldiers who close down training camps in foreign countries.

Terrorists are continually seeking ways to fund the purchase of costly products from legitimate laboratories. They set up false bank accounts and construct false identities, claiming to be scientists working in research institutes, sometimes in countries abroad. Careful screening of all requests helps identify the potential terrorist or the supply of products to those with malicious or criminal intent.

Nowhere is the **containment** of harmful products more carefully controlled than in the nuclear industry. It is with nuclear weapons that terrorists could achieve the largest number of dead and injured. The effects of nuclear attack are the most dramatic and would cause widespread horror throughout the world.

The trading in bomb-making materials is known to exist, and people have been caught trying to sell stolen quantities of uranium to known terrorist groups. A major problem is the poor economic state of the former Soviet republics. When communism in Russia collapsed in 1991, the country was in a poor state. Government and law enforcement were in chaos. A lot of nuclear weapons were left to rust, and some were stolen. There was little money, or interest, by the Russian authorities in doing anything about the situation.

As part of Exercise Sea Saber, nuclear, biological, and chemical disposal technicians from the 1st Marine 1st battalion prepare to search a U.S. Navy vessel in the Arabian Sea, January 2004.

In the United States, Senator Sam Nunn helped create a financial program to help the Russians dismantle their unneeded nuclear materials. Many weapons, stockpiles, and dumps were located in countries outside Russia, in states that were once part of the Soviet Union. These are in an even worse position economically.

Some material for making bombs is known to have found its way out of these former Soviet states. In the months just before 9/11, Osama bin Laden met with a Pakistani nuclear scientist, Sultan Bashirudden Mahmoud. Bin Laden told the scientist he had nuclear bomb-making

U.S. Senator Sam Nunn talks to the press at the NBC studios about the threat and prevention of nuclear terrorism, May 2005.

materials and wanted to know how to put the bomb together. In all, there are approximately 1,630 tons (1,485 metric tons) of bomb-grade uranium in research facilities, weapons dumps, and storage sites in 24 countries, of which 240 tons (219 metric tons) is on territory of the former Soviet Union.

Since the collapse of the communist system, there have been 700 reported attempted thefts of nuclear materials, all with the object of getting money for this high-priced bomb-making material. In 1998 Russian intelligence uncovered a plan to steal 40 pounds (18 kg) of bomb-grade uranium from a nuclear facility at Chelyabinsk and sell it on the black market. With this amount of material a skilled engineer could put together a small bomb.

In the two years between 2002 and 2004, teams of international specialists have retrieved more than 231 pounds (105 kg) of bomb-grade uranium from Uzbekistan, Bulgaria, Romania, Libya, and the Czech Republic.

The accidental 1986 explosion at the nuclear reactor at Chernobyl in the Ukraine showed how radiation could travel far distances.

Chapter Six

The Super-weapon

Apart from enriched uranium warheads made in centrifuges and the more costly plutonium bomb-making process, there is another, potentially much more lethal, bomb. Nuclear bombs are capable of producing a tremendous blast followed seconds later by an intense pulse of heat. If the blast fails to kill you, the heat will.

Beyond the blast and heat zone, intense radiation poisons the body, and people die over the next several hours, days, and weeks. After that, radioactive dust and particles travel around the Earth in the atmosphere on winds that gradually bring them down to the ground, contaminating even more people in distant areas.

Scientists know that nuclear bombs can be speeded up, increasing the blast and minimizing radiation. Or they can be slowed down, reducing the blast and increasing the radiation. Slow-burning bombs of this kind were considered during the 1980s. It was said that the military value of such a bomb was that it could be used against Soviet invasion troops in cities without buildings needing to be completely destroyed.

Osama bin Laden, leader of Al Qaeda, has long sought to get hold of weapons of mass destruction.

Such a bomb would have had very little blast, but would have released massive bursts of extremely intense radiation that would have destroyed the enemy. There would have been the dead, the dying, and the intensely sick—effects no invading army wants to experience.

Pressure against the morality of using such weapons outlawed their use. It was felt justifiable to use a blast weapon but not one that deliberately poisoned the enemy, dooming them individually to a horrible and lingering death.

Yet it is precisely this kind of "dirty bomb" that terrorists, seemingly without moral conscience, may find attractive for their purposes. A dirty bomb could be made with considerably less effort than it takes to put together a uranium bomb, much less a plutonium bomb.

However, the means of getting any nuclear bomb to its target poses serious problems. The usual way is to attach it to a long-range missile or drop it from a bomber. Terrorists do not have access to either. Even the biggest missile developed by Saddam Hussein was incapable of reaching any target outside the Middle East, let alone western Europe, the Far East, or the United States.

Yet a dirty bomb could be carried into any U.S. harbor—New York, San Diego, or Boston, for example—and be detonated from a boat. Such a bomb would be about the size of a small office desk and could be triggered by a suicide bomber.

The effects of such a bomb would be unimaginable. The blast would be great, about the magnitude of a 10-ton (9.1-metric ton) high-explosive bomb. The heat and radiation, however, would be so intense that everyone within a radius of 5 miles (8 km) would die almost immediately. At a radius of 10 miles (16 km), sickness would set in within a few hours, and people would start to die on the second day. About two-thirds of those would

A "dirty bomb" could be smuggled into the country in a container. This mobile truck X-ray machine is used to check incoming containers.

die within a week, the rest within a month. At a radius of 20 miles (32 km), about half the people would contract sicknesses such as leukemia and die within a year.

Beyond that radius untold numbers would contract blood diseases and be genetically damaged, unable to bear children and

Working hard to protect New York City from terrorist attack, the U.S. Coast Guard is one of our first lines of defense.

In the hunt for chemical, biological, and nuclear weapons many different defense methods are used. This sniffer dog at the Customs and Border Protection Canine Enforcement Center is trained to detect dangerous chemicals.

incapable of ever leading normal lives. The total numbers of people affected from a dirty bomb detonated in New York harbor on a weekday in office buildings all full could be as high as 3 million, 1 million of whom would die.

The consequences of such an attack would be devastating, and the effects would continue far beyond the present generation. Attacks using weapons of mass destruction would be far worse than anything we have experienced to date.

Such is the nature of the threat we face. Vigilance and firm measures to eliminate a new generation of terrorists is a major priority for this nation and every civilized country.

Glossary

aerosol: a fine spray

alchemist: a medieval scientist who tried to turn base metals, like iron, into gold

anthrax: a serious infectious disease that can be lethal for humans

antibiotic: a drug that is used to kill bacteria and help cure diseases

biologist: a person who studies living things such as plants and animals

centrifuge: a machine that is used to separate substances

chemist: a person who studies chemistry

containment: stopping something from happening

deterrent: something that is used to stop someone from doing something

detonate: to set off an explosion

dissemination: when something is dispersed or spread out

enzyme: a substance produced by humans and animals that speeds up chemical reactions

fluorine: a poisonous gas that causes severe burns when it comes into contact with skin

genetic: describes the ways personal characteristics are passed down from one generation to another through genes

leach: to drain a chemical out of something

modification: the changing of something

perpetrator: the person who is responsible for carrying out an action

phosgene: a poisonous gas developed before World War II

physicist: someone who studies the science of physics, including energy, heat, movement, sound, and light

plutonium: a substance that can be used to make nuclear weapons

replicate: to produce an exact copy of something

rickettsiae: a group of very small bacteria that cause diseases in humans

sarin: a nerve gas

toxic: poisonous

vaccine: a substance which can be injected into a person to prevent them catching a disease.

victim: someone who suffers or dies because of someone else's actions

virulent: something that is very severe or harmful

virus: a living thing that multiplies within body cells, often causing diseases

Further Reading

Binns, Tristan. *The CIA (Government Agencies)*. Sagebrush, 2002

Binns, Tristan. *The FBI (Government Agencies)*. Sagebrush, 2002

Brennan, Kristine. *The Chernobyl Nuclear Disaster (Great Disasters)*. Chelsea House, 2002

Campbell, Geoffrey A. *A Vulnerable America (Lucent Library of Homeland Security)*. Lucent, 2003

Donovan, Sandra. *How Government Works: Protecting America*. Lerner Publishing Group, 2004

Gow, Mary. *Attack on America: The Day the Twin Towers Collapsed (American Disasters)*. Enslow Publishers, 2002

Hasan, Tahara. *Anthrax Attacks Around the World (Terrorist Attacks)*. Rosen Publishing Group, 2003

Katz, Samuel M. *Global Counterstrike: International Counterterrorism (Terrorist Dossiers)*. Lerner Publishing Group, 2004

Katz, Samuel M. *Targeting Terror: Counterterrorist Raids (Terrorist Dossiers)*. Lerner Publishing Group, 2004

Katz, Samuel M. *U.S. Counterstrike: American Counterterrorism (Terrorist Dossiers)*. Lerner Publishing Group, 2004

Margulies, Phillip. *Al-Qaeda: Osama Bin Laden's Army of Terrorists (Inside the World's Most Infamous Terrorist Organizations)*. Rosen Publishing Group, 2003

Marquette, Scott. *America Under Attack (America at War)*. Rourke Publishing LLC, 2003

Morris, Neil. *The Atlas of Islam*. Barron's, 2003

Owen, David. *Hidden Secrets: A Complete History of Espionage and the Technology Used to Support It*. Firefly Books Ltd, 2002

Ritchie, Jason. *Iraq and the Fall of Saddam Hussein*. Oliver Press, 2003

Websites to visit

The Central Intelligence Agency:
www.cia.gov

The Department of Defense:
www.defenselink.mil

The Department of Homeland Security:
www.dhs.gov

The Federal Bureau of Investigation:
www.fbi.gov

The U.S. Air Force:
www.af.mil

The U.S. Army
www.army.mil

The U.S. Coast Guard:
www.uscg.mil

The U.S. Government Official Website:
www.firstgov.gov

The U.S. Marine Corps:
www.usmc.mil

The U.S. Navy:
www.navy.mil

The U.S. Secret Service:
www.secretservice.gov

The White House:
www.whitehouse.gov

Index